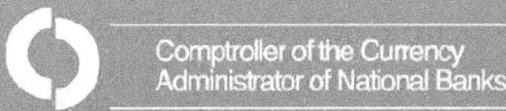

Comptroller of the Currency
Administrator of National Banks

US Department of the Treasury

I0439634

2012 Survey of Credit Underwriting Practices

Office of the Comptroller of the Currency
Washington, D.C.

June 2012

Contents

Introduction

The Office of the Comptroller of the Currency (OCC) conducted its 18th annual "Survey of Credit Underwriting Practices" to identify trends in lending standards and credit risk for the most common types of commercial and retail credit offered by national banks and federal savings associations. Federal savings associations (FSA) are included for the first time in this year's survey. Results for national banks and FSAs were generally consistent; therefore, results are presented in aggregate across both institution types. The survey covers the 12-month period ending February 29, 2012.

The 2012 survey presents OCC examiner assessments of credit underwriting standards at 87 banks with assets of $3 billion or more. Examiners reported on loan products for each company whose loan volume was 2 percent or more of its committed loan portfolio—or $10 billion or more in committed exposure. The OCC recognizes that banks may offer many other loan products not meeting these thresholds because of the size of the product portfolios; however, examiners did not gather information on them for this report. The survey covers loans totaling $4.6 trillion as of December 31, 2011, representing 91 percent of total loans in the national banking and FSA system at that time. Large banks discussed in this report are the 18 largest banks by asset size supervised by the OCC's Large Bank Supervision Department; the other 69 banks are supervised by the OCC's Midsize and Community Bank Supervision Department.

OCC examiners assigned to each bank assessed overall credit trends for 18 commercial and retail credit products. For the purposes of this survey, commercial credit includes 11 categories:

- Agricultural
- Asset-based lending
- Commercial construction
- Commercial leasing
- International
- Large corporate
- Leveraged
- Middle market
- Other commercial real estate
- Residential construction
- Small business

Retail credit includes seven categories:

- Affordable housing
- Conventional home equity
- Credit cards
- High loan-to-value (HLTV) home equity
- Indirect consumer paper
- Direct consumer
- Residential first mortgages

Underwriting standards, as used in this report, refers to the terms and conditions under which banks extend or renew credit, such as financial and collateral requirements, repayment programs, maturities, pricing, and covenants. Conclusions about easing or tightening represent OCC examiners' observations during the 12-month survey period ending February 29, 2012. A conclusion that underwriting standards for a particular loan category eased or tightened does not necessarily indicate an adjustment in all of the standards for that particular product. Rather, the conclusion indicates that the adjustments that did occur had the net effect of easing or tightening the aggregate conditions under which banks extended credit.

Part I of this report summarizes the overall findings of the survey. Part II shows the findings in data tables and graphs. Part III presents the raw data used to develop the survey's principal findings and to create the data tables and graphs. (Note: Some percentages in tables and graphs do not add to 100 because of rounding.)

Part I: Overall Results

Primary Findings

- The results of this year's survey showed that underwriting standards remained largely unchanged from last year, although some easing was noted within certain commercial and retail products. OCC examiners reported that national banks and FSAs (collectively, banks) that eased standards generally did so in response to changes in economic outlook, the competitive environment, and the bank's risk appetite, including a desire for growth. Large banks reported the highest share of eased underwriting standards.

- Loan portfolios that experienced the most easing in underwriting standards include indirect consumer, credit cards, large corporate, asset-based lending, and leveraged loans. Loan portfolios that experienced the most tightening in underwriting since last year include HLTV home equity, international, commercial and residential construction, affordable housing, and residential real estate loans.

- As in the past, the economy's health was a major factor influencing changes in underwriting standards. Expectations regarding the future health of the economy, however, differ by bank and loan product as examiners reported that economic outlook was one of the main reasons given for easing or tightening underwriting standards. Other factors influencing tighter underwriting standards were changes in risk appetite and product performance. Factors contributing to eased standards were changes in the competitive environment, increased competition and desire for growth, and increased market liquidity.

- The tightening previously seen in small business banking underwriting practices has decreased with 82 percent of banks now reporting unchanged standards from the last survey. The level of credit risk in small business loans remained stable, and is expected to remain so over the next 12 months.

- Since the 2011 survey, changes in the level of credit risk were mixed in commercial and retail portfolios. Approximately 18 percent of commercial and retail loan products showed increased credit risk, 32 percent indicated decreased credit risk, and 50 percent showed the same level of credit risk when compared with 12 months ago. Over the next 12 months, examiners believe that credit risk will likely increase for 25 percent of the loan products, decrease for 24 percent, and remain unchanged for 51 percent.

- Similar to the 2011 survey results, this year's survey indicated that the majority of banks generally apply the same underwriting standards to loans underwritten with the intent to hold as to those underwritten with the intent to sell.

Commentary on Credit Risk

Because of the significant volume of commercial real estate (CRE), residential real estate, and home equity loans in banks, the greatest source of credit risk in banks was the general economic weakness and its resultant impact on real estate values. Credit risk in the credit card portfolios has leveled off but remains significant because of the effects of the weak economy and high unemployment.

The uncertain economy, desire for loan growth, competition, and credit culture were listed by examiners as the most important credit-related issues for banks. In the aftermath of the financial crisis, some banks continued to have elevated credit risk exposure, and many banks continue to struggle with high levels of problem credits, declining collateral values, and uncertainty about the economic outlook. In response, those banks generally have either tightened or left their underwriting standards unchanged. Some banks have begun to ease underwriting standards in certain products to meet loan demand, remain competitive, and improve earnings. In large banks, leveraged lending is showing moderate easing from tighter underwriting standards in place during the financial crisis. This change is due to increased competition, expanding market liquidity, and desire to grow and improve margins.

As banks begin easing underwriting standards to meet loan demand and improve earnings, they should maintain prudent underwriting standards. The OCC expects banks to underwrite loans based on sound underwriting standards, regardless of the intent to hold or sell the loan, and to apply the same general standards for both types of lending.

Overall, examiners reported a balance between easing and tightening of underwriting standards, with the majority of standards remaining unchanged (70 percent for commercial and 63 percent for retail). Easing of overall commercial underwriting standards was reported in 14 percent of the banks, and easing of overall retail underwriting standards in 15 percent of the banks. Loan products that experienced the most easing were indirect consumer, large corporate, asset-based lending, credit cards, and leveraged loans. Commercial underwriting standards tightened in 16 percent of the banks, and retail underwriting standards tightened in 22 percent of the banks. Loan products with the most tightening were HLTV home equity, international, commercial and residential construction, affordable housing, and residential real estate.

Pricing was the primary method that banks used to ease underwriting standards for commercial products. Changes in collateral requirements and score card cutoffs were used to ease underwriting standards for retail products. For banks that tightened standards, loan covenants (except leverage) and collateral requirements were most frequently used to tighten commercial standards, while score cards, documentation and collateral requirements were used to tighten retail standards. In most products, examiners reported fewer approved exceptions to policy.

The survey indicates that 77 percent of examiner responses reflected that the overall level of credit risk will either remain unchanged or improve over the next 12 months. This represents an increase from last year's survey, which showed that 64 percent of the responses showed an expectation for an improvement in the level of credit risk over the next 12 months. In instances when examiners expect risk to increase, their primary reasons were the state of the economy, high levels of problem loans, competition, and continued downward pressure on real estate values.

Commercial Underwriting Standards

The number of banks where examiners report a net easing in commercial credit standards declined from 2011. As presented in table 1, the survey results indicate most banks (70 percent) show unchanged underwriting while 14 percent of banks eased underwriting standards. The easing in underwriting indicates increased competition and a desire for loan growth. The easing of standards occurred mainly in large banks.

Table 1: Overall Commercial Product Underwriting Trends

	2006	2007	2008	2009	2010	2011	2012
Eased	31%	26%	6%	0%	2%	20%	14%
Unchanged	63%	58%	42%	14%	33%	48%	70%
Tightened	6%	16%	52%	86%	65%	32%	16%

For additional information, see figure 1 on page 13.

Examiners reported that the predominant reasons for easing and tightening underwriting standards include increased competition and a desire for loan growth as well as changes in risk appetite, portfolio quality, and economic outlook. Examiners also reported that banks have mixed expectations for the future; some banks cited improving economic outlook as a reason for easing underwriting standards, while others cited an uncertain economic outlook for tightening standards. Examiners reported changes in risk appetite and in the competitive environment as the primary reasons for tightening standards. Increased market liquidity, competition, product performance, and, to a lesser degree, change in risk appetite were primary reasons for easing standards. The return of liquidity in secondary markets was a key contributor to easing standards in leveraged finance, asset-based loans, international, and certain commercial real estate products.

In this year's survey, pricing, increased credit availability, lengthening maturities, and fewer or relaxed loan covenants indicated increased competition for certain commercial loan products. This contrasts with previous years, when tightened pricing and loan fees were more evident. As the economy recovers and competition increases, the OCC expects banks to maintain prudent underwriting standards.

Notwithstanding these trends, examiners cited good or acceptable adherence to underwriting standards; they also cited well-supported exceptions for most products. The level of approved exceptions decreased in 23 percent of commercial products, while 69 percent indicated no change in the volume of approved exceptions. Underwriting exception tracking is in place for 92 percent of the loan products.

Selected Product Trends

Underwriting standards tightened for some commercial loan products and eased for others. The most prevalent tightening occurred in CRE and international loans. Easing was identified in leveraged, large corporate, and asset-based lending. Large banks typically offered the products with the most easing.

The direction of credit risk across the 87 banks moved from a mix of increasing, unchanged, and decreasing to largely unchanged or decreasing, as examiners expect the risk levels for 2013 to decrease or remain unchanged. Examiner expectations are consistent with broad trends in commercial credit quality, which generally show stabilization or improvement even though credit quality indicators remain at elevated levels. International and residential construction reflected moderately increasing levels of credit risk, while leasing, CRE, and leveraged loans reflected significant net decreasing levels of risk responses.

CRE

CRE products include residential construction, commercial construction, and all other CRE loans. Almost all surveyed banks offered at least one type of CRE product. CRE remains a primary concern of examiners given the current economic environment and some banks' significant concentrations in this product relative to their capital. While the majority of banks' underwriting standards remained unchanged for CRE, tightening continued in residential construction and commercial (21 percent and 20 percent, respectively). Easing was noted in commercial real estate—other, with 12 percent showing eased standards. Examiners cited the distressed real estate market, poor product performance, reduced risk appetite, and change in market strategy as the main reasons for banks' net tightening.

The level and direction of credit risk in CRE continued to show improvement. All products showed some level of increasing risk, but the majority of examiners' responses noted declining or unchanged risk. Increased credit risks were attributed to continued economic weakness and a slow recovery, concerns with the current and anticipated levels of problem loans, anticipated portfolio growth, and slowing ability to improve problem loan levels. Examiners noted moderate-to-strong progress in banks' ability to work out problem loans, loan sales and portfolio reductions, and stable-to-improving economic conditions. Tables 2, 3, and 4 provide breakdowns by real estate type.

Nineteen banks (22 percent) offered residential construction loan products. Recent performance of these products has generally been poor, and many banks have either exited the product or significantly curtailed new originations. Poor initial underwriting, compounded by weak economic conditions, resulted in high levels of problem loans and losses. Table 2 shows that underwriting standards for 79 percent of banks offering the product in 2012 were unchanged for residential construction; 21 percent of banks tightened standards. None reported easing standards.

Table 2: CRE Lending: Residential Construction

	2006	2007	2008	2009	2010	2011	2012
Eased	25%	17%	2%	0%	0%	0%	0%
Unchanged	64%	50%	36%	8%	36%	63%	79%
Tightened	11%	33%	62%	92%	64%	37%	21%

For additional information, see tables on page 29.

Thirty-four banks (39 percent) offered commercial construction loans. The economic environment adversely affected collateral values which have not stabilized in many areas. Table 3 shows that underwriting standards for commercial construction remain unchanged at 75 percent of banks; 20 percent of banks offering commercial construction tightened underwriting standards; and five percent eased standards.

Table 3: CRE Lending: Commercial Construction

	2006	2007	2008	2009	2010	2011	2012
Eased	32%	28%	8%	0%	3%	3%	5%
Unchanged	56%	59%	43%	20%	25%	61%	75%
Tightened	12%	13%	49%	80%	72%	36%	20%

For additional information, see tables on page 28.

Seventy-three banks (84 percent) offered a variety of CRE loans for purposes other than residential or commercial construction. For purposes of this survey, the OCC broadly grouped these loans under an "other" category. As with commercial residential and commercial construction loans, the survey showed that the economic environment and depressed collateral values continued to affect risk in this loan category. Table 4 shows that 12 percent of banks offering "other" CRE loans tightened underwriting standards, while 12 percent eased standards and 76 percent left underwriting standards unchanged.

Table 4: CRE Lending: Other

	2006	2007	2008	2009	2010	2011	2012
Eased	32%	20%	2%	2%	2%	9%	12%
Unchanged	60%	73%	73%	22%	38%	58%	76%
Tightened	8%	7%	25%	76%	60%	33%	12%

For additional information, see tables on page 30.

Leveraged Loans

While only 13 large or midsize banks (15 percent) offered leveraged loans, the size of the portfolio is significant relative to all loans due to dollar size. Table 5 shows that 38 percent of banks offering leveraged loans eased underwriting standards; none reported tightening standards; and 62 percent of the banks left underwriting standards unchanged. Easing is attributed to increased competition, changing economic conditions, risk appetite, and improved market liquidity. This is the second consecutive year for which examiners reported substantial easing.

Examiners also reported that the level of credit risk in leveraged loans decreased in 54 percent of banks offering leveraged loans and remained unchanged in 38 percent. Eight percent reported that credit risk increased somewhat. Examiners expect that over the next year the credit risk in this product will likely remain unchanged or increase in 77 percent of the banks offering the product. Any increase would be due to competition and increasing market liquidity driven by banks' and investors' pursuit of growth in earning assets. Examiners will monitor this expected trend closely, as such pressures could result in easing underwriting standards, lower pricing, and fewer covenants.

Table 5: Leveraged Loans

	2006	2007	2008	2009	2010	2011	2012
Eased	61%	67%	20%	0%	0%	37%	38%
Unchanged	31%	33%	20%	31%	25%	44%	62%
Tightened	8%	0%	60%	69%	75%	19%	0%

For additional information, see tables on page 33.

Small Business Loans

Forty-four of the surveyed banks (51 percent) offer small business loans. Underwriting standards remained unchanged at 82 percent of the banks offering the product. The remaining banks eased or tightened standards by 9 percent. Changes in economic outlook, risk appetite, market liquidity, and portfolio performance were the primary reasons for changes in credit underwriting. Notwithstanding the 9 percent of banks that eased standards, examiners indicate current underwriting standards at all banks remained either conservative at 44 percent or moderate at 53 percent.

Examiners indicate that small business credit risk declined or remained relatively unchanged at 84 percent of the banks and expect the risk will continue to decline or remain the same over the next year in 84 percent of the banks offering the product. Changes in external conditions and portfolio quality were most frequently reported as reasons for the reduced level of risk.

Table 6: Small Business Loans

	2006	2007	2008	2009	2010	2011	2012
Eased	19%	11%	11%	0%	0%	12%	9%
Unchanged	76%	76%	72%	36%	34%	55%	82%
Tightened	5%	13%	17%	64%	66%	33%	9%

For additional information, see tables on page 35.

Originate to Hold Versus Originate to Sell

The OCC expects banks to underwrite loans based on sound underwriting standards, regardless of the intent to hold or sell loans, and to apply the same general standards for both types of lending.

Of the loan products surveyed, 17 percent were originated to sell; the largest categories of loans in this group were large corporate loans, leveraged loans, international credits, and asset-based loans. Examiners noted different standards for loans originated to hold versus loans originated to sell in 1 of 31 banks offering large corporate loans, 2 of 13 banks offering leveraged loans, and 1 of 11 banks offering international loans. As shown in table 7, there has been continued improvement since 2008 in reducing the differences in hold versus sell underwriting standards. The OCC continues to monitor and assess any differences in underwriting standards for loans that banks intend to sell versus those they intend to hold.

Table 7: Hold versus Sell Underwriting Standards

Product	Underwritten differently				
	2008	2009	2010	2011	2012
Leveraged loans	67%	38%	12%	13%	15%
International	40%	0%	10%	11%	9%
Large corporate	21%	21%	3%	3%	3%
CRE—other	20%	9%	0%	0%	1%
Asset-based loans	33%	13%	0%	0%	0%
CRE—residential construction	17%	17%	0%	0%	0%
CRE—commercial construction	20%	10%	0%	0%	0%

Retail Underwriting Standards

Each of the 87 banks in the survey underwrites one or more of the seven retail loan products, with residential real estate loans being the largest, distantly followed by home equity loans. Despite the increase since 2011 in the number of surveyed banks, the size of the retail portfolio among those banks did not change relative to the total portfolio of loans covered in the survey.

As shown in table 8, examiners reported a continued slow trend toward easing, but the majority (63 percent) of underwriting standards remains unchanged with 15 percent showing eased and 22 percent showing tightened standards. Examiners attributed the easing to improving economic trends, problem asset resolution, changes in the competitive environment, and product performance. Good or acceptable adherence to underwriting standards was noted, with exceptions well supported for the majority of products. Exception tracking is in place for 91 percent of the individual retail products, representing a decrease of 3 percent from 2011. Examiners report that 80 percent of the banks surveyed do not plan to introduce any new products during the next year and do not expect credit risk to increase in the retail products that they currently originate.

Table 8: Overall Retail Product Underwriting Trends

	2006	2007	2008	2009	2010	2011	2012
Eased	28%	20%	0%	0%	0%	7%	15%
Unchanged	65%	67%	32%	17%	26%	63%	63%
Tightened	7%	13%	68%	83%	74%	30%	22%

For additional information, see figure 7 on page 20.

The direction of credit risk for individual retail products showed further improvement from previous years, with examiners reporting unchanged or decreased credit risk at 82 percent of banks versus 68 percent in the previous year. In the next 12 months, examiners expect an increase in credit risk in 27 percent of banks, while 73 percent of banks are expected to incur decreased or unchanged levels of credit risk.

Examiners reported that the quantity of credit risk in the banks' retail portfolios was largely unchanged. Individual retail products that saw an increase in the quantity of credit risk were other direct consumer loans and residential real estate; the increase was primarily due to continued high unemployment and the fragility of the housing market. Although examiners reported the direction of risk increased in select individual retail products, the overall trend in credit risk levels improved from last year.

Examiners reported that the most important credit-related issues in retail products centered on the economic recovery (both on a national and regional basis), problem asset resolution, and housing related issues. Secondary issues varied. Examiners reported that community banks are anxious about expediting acquisitions under satisfactory risk management structures, maintaining access to high-quality loans, and responding to the pressure for growth. Midsize and large banks are focused on designing long-term strategic plans, managing portfolio risk, and dealing with competitive pressure to prudently ease credit standards.

Selected Product Trends

The following sections discuss changes within various product types.

Residential Real Estate

Eighty-four of the surveyed banks (97 percent) originated residential real estate loans. As shown in table 9, there is a slow continued trend from tightening to unchanged standards, with 65 percent of the banks reporting unchanged residential real estate underwriting standards. Despite the many challenges and uncertainties presented by the housing market, none of the banks exited the residential real estate business during the past year; however, examiners reported that two banks plan to exit the business in the coming year. Additionally, examiners indicated that the quantity of risk inherent in these portfolios remained unchanged or decreased at 81 percent of the banks.

As shown in table 10, similar results were noted for conventional home equity loans, with 68 percent of banks keeping underwriting standards unchanged, and 18 percent easing standards. Since the 2011 survey, of the six banks that originated high loan-to-value home equity loans, three banks have exited the business and one plans to exit the business in the coming year.

Table 9: Residential Real Estate Lending

	2006	2007	2008	2009	2010	2011	2012
Eased	26%	19%	0%	0%	5%	8%	10%
Unchanged	69%	67%	44%	27%	36%	52%	65%
Tightened	5%	14%	56%	73%	59%	40%	25%

For additional information, see tables on page 42.

Table 10: Conventional Home Equity

	2006	2007	2008	2009	2010	2011	2012
Eased	34%	19%	2%	0%	5%	9%	18%
Unchanged	64%	65%	46%	22%	35%	55%	68%
Tightened	2%	16%	52%	78%	60%	36%	14%

For additional information, see tables on page 37.

Table 11: High Loan-to-Value Home Equity

	2006	2007	2008	2009	2010	2011	2012
Eased	37%	22%	6%	0%	0%	0%	17%
Unchanged	63%	61%	6%	7%	13%	50%	17%
Tightened	0%	17%	88%	93%	87%	50%	66%

For additional information, see tables on page 40.

Credit Cards

Twenty of the surveyed banks (23 percent) offered credit cards. Table 12 shows the continued significant easing of credit card underwriting standards by 35 percent. Examiners attributed the easing of standards to changes in economic outlook, product performance, competitive environment, risk appetite, and market strategy. The primary methods used for easing credit underwriting standards were changes in pricing and fees, scorecard cutoffs, and debt-to-income ratios.

Credit risk in the card portfolios has stabilized; examiners reported no change in the level of credit risk at 50 percent of the banks and a decrease at 45 percent of the banks. In the next 12 months, examiners expect no change in the level of credit risk at 60 percent of the banks. Examiners reported increased exposure to credit cards at three banks since the last survey and noted plans to significantly increase exposure at six banks in the next 12 months. However, examiners reported being somewhat concerned with the direction of credit risk at 50 percent of the banks. This concern is supported to a degree with one company planning to exit this line of business in the coming year. Examiners noted that increased competition from new companies and "re-entrants" is forcing continued easing of standards in order to maintain market share.

Table 12: Credit Card Lending

	2006	2007	2008	2009	2010	2011	2012
Eased	19%	16%	18%	0%	0%	25%	35%
Unchanged	56%	79%	47%	32%	19%	31%	50%
Tightened	25%	5%	35%	68%	81%	44%	15%

For additional information, see tables on page 38.

Consumer Lending (Direct and Indirect)

Direct and indirect consumer lending encompasses a variety of products, with banks taking different actions with regard to underwriting standards or plans for each product in this section. Indirect lending is generally dominated by auto loans but can also include other products such as student, marine, and recreational vehicle loans. Examiners' conclusions about credit risk or the direction of credit risk may not be the same for all products grouped in this section. When differences exist, the response generally relates to the most significant product by dollar volume.

During the survey period, 25 banks (29 percent) and 20 banks (23 percent) participated in direct and indirect lending, respectively. As shown in table 13, underwriting standards eased in 12 percent of the 25 direct lending banks, while 88 percent of those banks kept their standards unchanged. None tightened standards. Table 14 shows 60 percent of banks continued significant easing in underwriting standards for indirect lending. The easing was attributed to changes in the competitive environment, market strategy, and risk appetite. The underwriting standards that changed for these products are primarily pricing and fees, collateral requirements, advance rates, maximum maturity, scorecard cutoffs, and debt-to-income. Thirty-five percent of banks' standards remained unchanged, while 5 percent tightened standards.

Table 13: Direct Consumer Lending

	2006	2007	2008	2009	2010	2011	2012
Eased	3%	8%	6%	4%	0%	10%	12%
Unchanged	91%	87%	72%	28%	68%	75%	88%
Tightened	6%	5%	22%	68%	32%	15%	0%

For additional information, see tables on page 39.

Table 14: Indirect Consumer Lending

	2006	2007	2008	2009	2010	2011	2012
Eased	35%	16%	20%	0%	5%	37%	60%
Unchanged	52%	75%	56%	26%	33%	47%	35%
Tightened	13%	9%	24%	74%	62%	16%	5%

For additional information, see tables on page 41.

The survey showed that the expected level of credit risk in the indirect portfolio is expected to increase somewhat at 45 percent of the banks in the next 12 months. The primary reasons for increased risk are changes in underwriting standards, external conditions, risk selection, and underwriting practices. Sixteen percent of the banks participating in direct consumer lending and 30 percent of those originating indirect consumer lending plan on increasing their exposure to these products in the coming year.

Originate to Hold Versus Originate to Sell

Banks originated 76 percent of retail products to hold, while the balance was originated to sell. The most popular retail product to sell was residential real estate loans, while the most common product to hold was conventional home equity loans. The OCC continues to monitor and assess any difference in underwriting standards for loans that banks intend to hold versus those they intend to sell.

Part II: Data Graphs

Some percentages used to create the data graphs do not add to 100 because of rounding.

Figure 1: Overall Commercial Credit Underwriting Trends (Percentage of Responses)

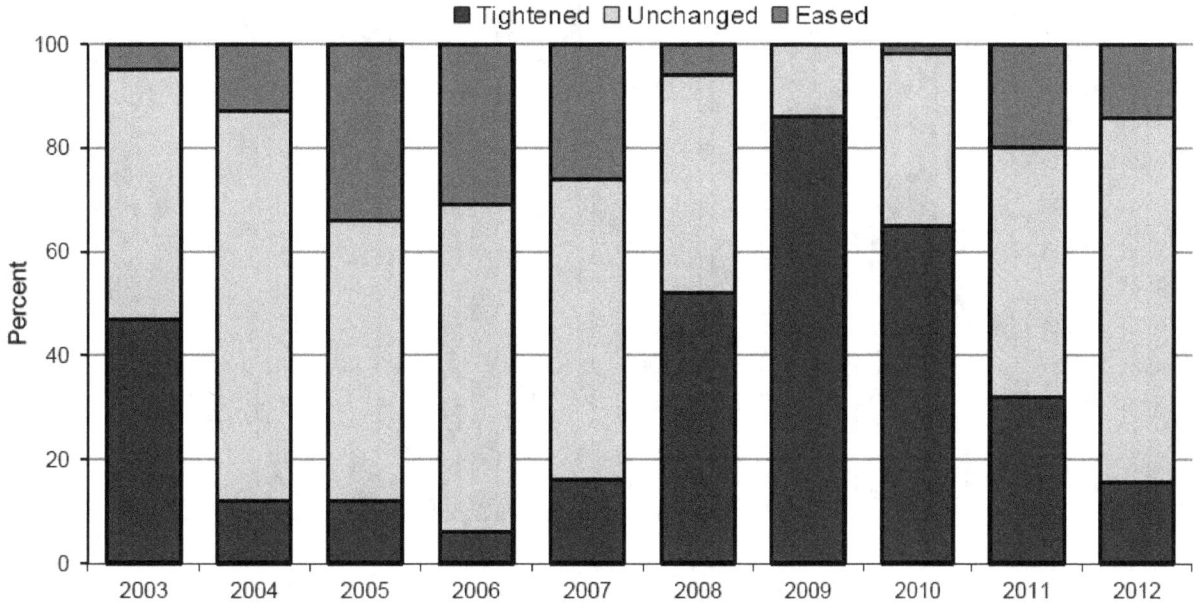

Figure 2: Commercial Underwriting Trends, by Product Type (Percentage of Responses)

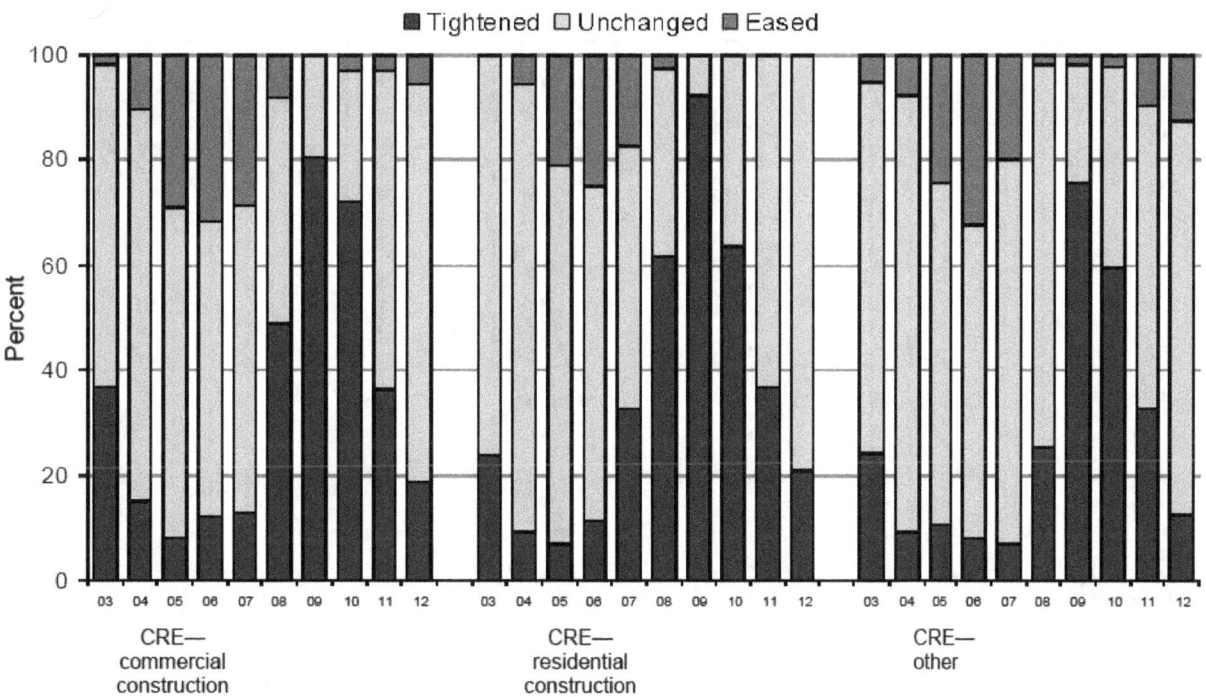

Figure 2 (cont.): Commercial Underwriting Trends, by Product Type (Percentage of Responses)

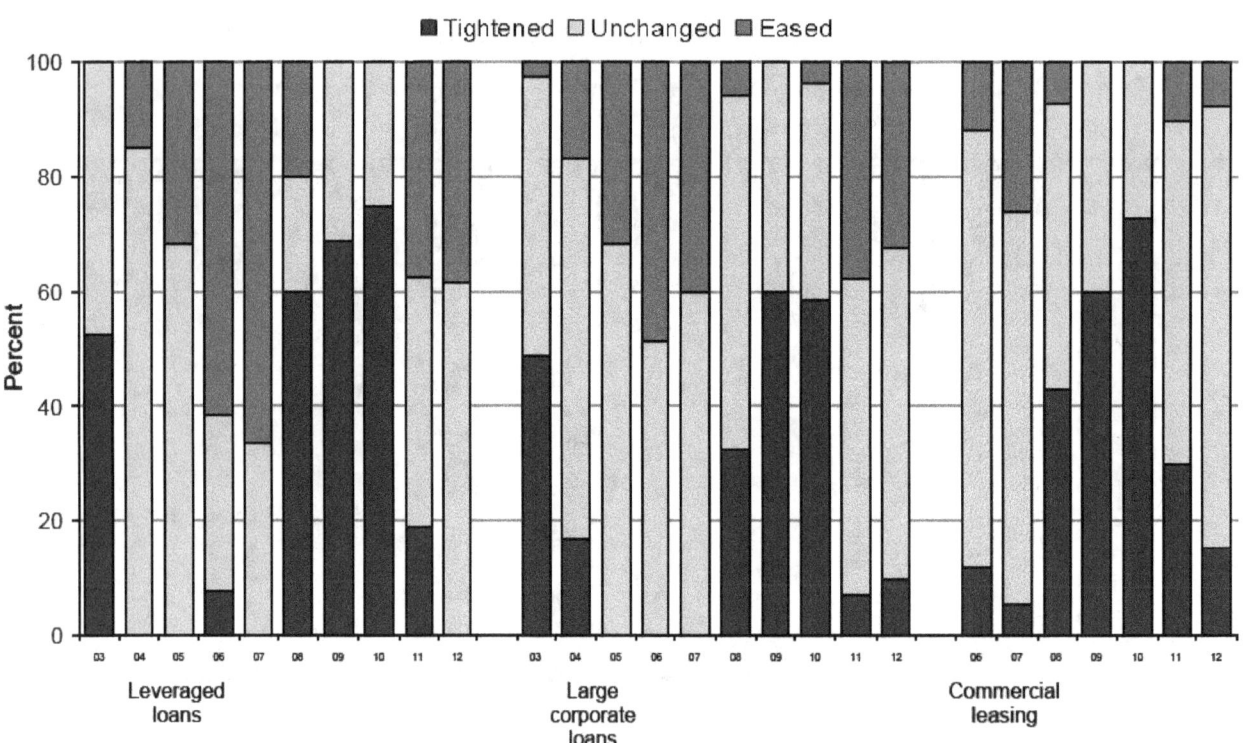

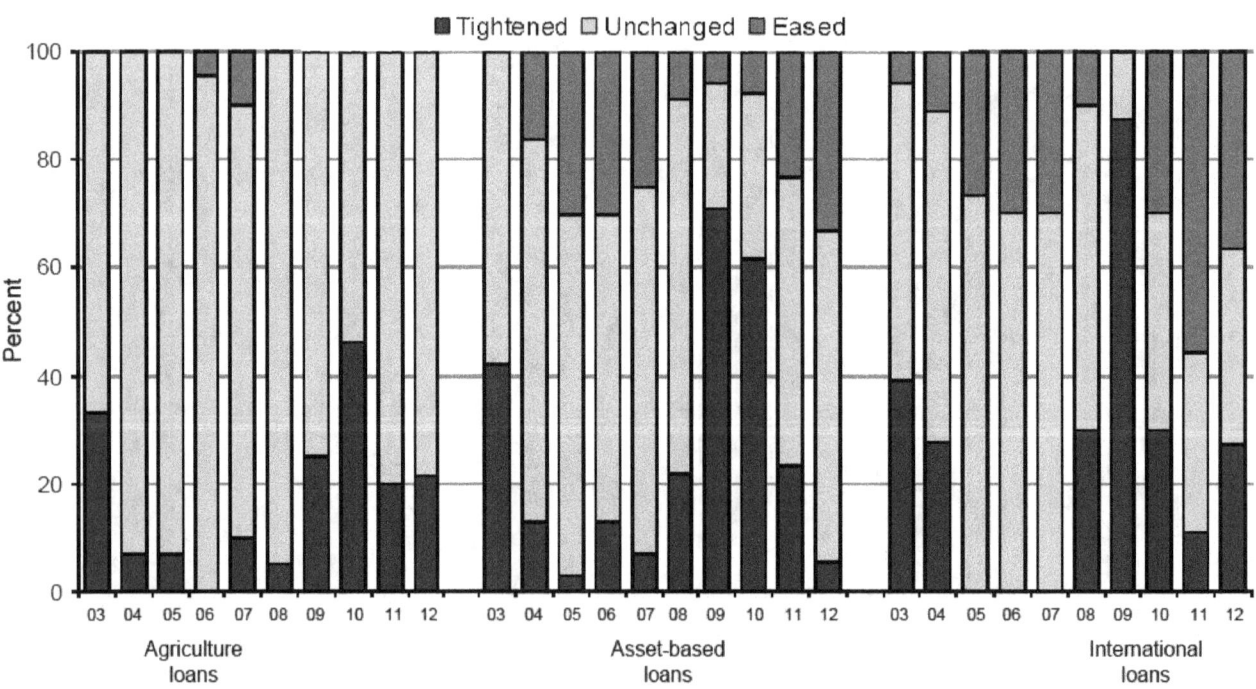

Figure 2 (cont.): Commercial Underwriting Trends, by Product Type (Percentage of Responses)

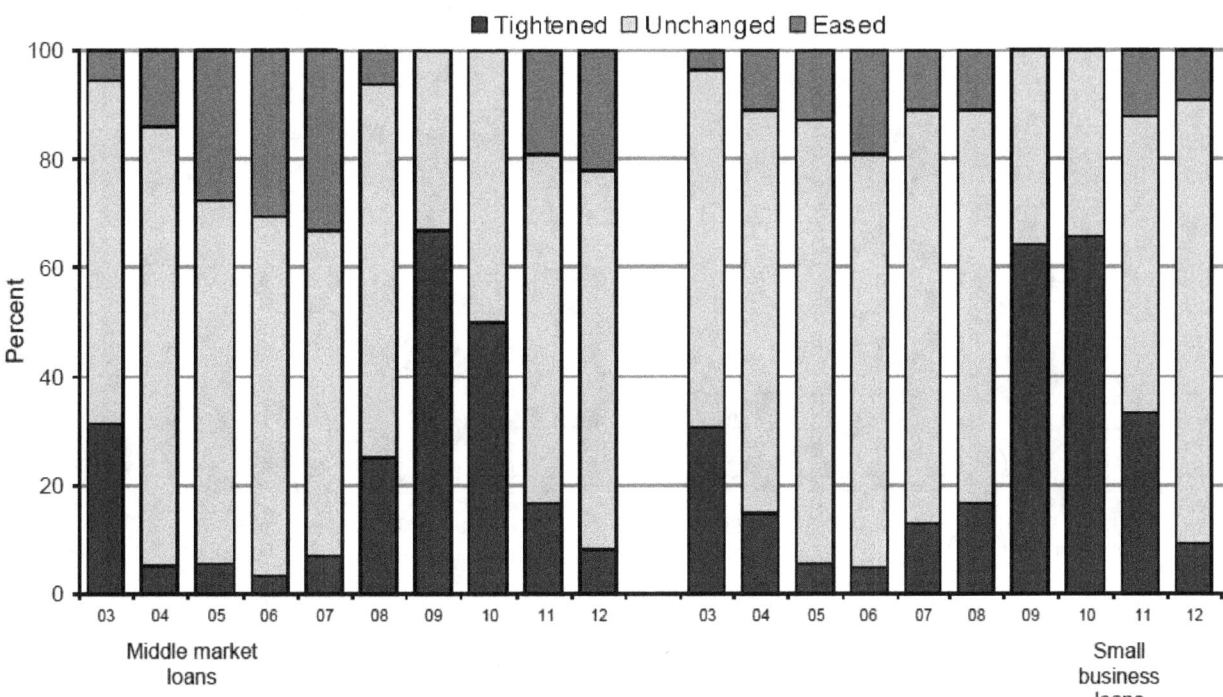

Figure 3: Reasons for Changing Commercial Underwriting Standards

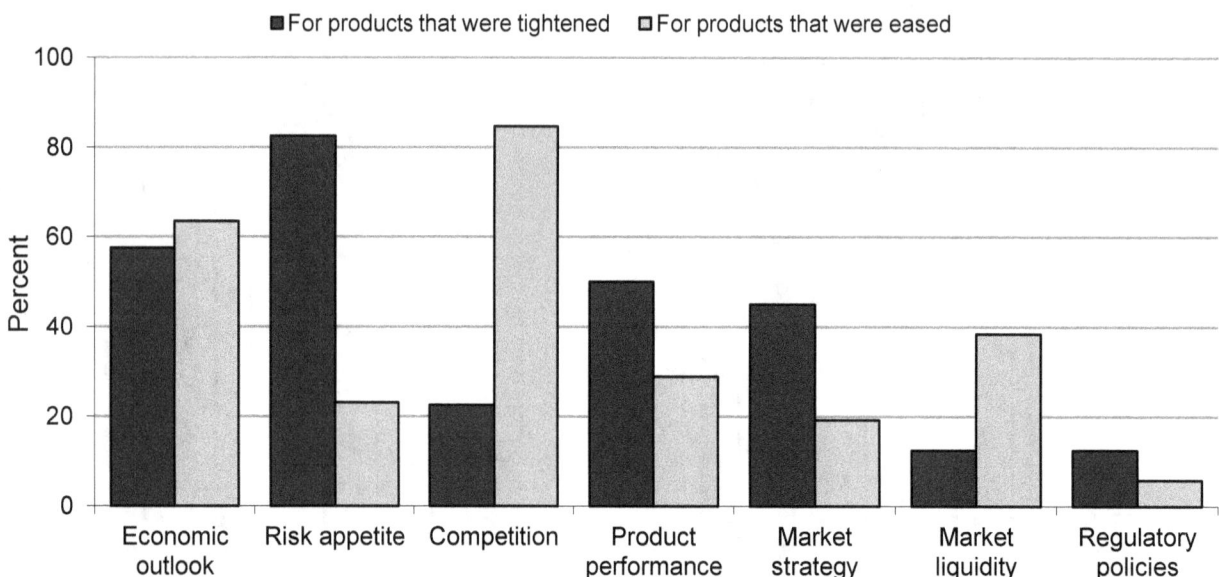

Figure 4: Methods Used to Change Commercial Underwriting Standards

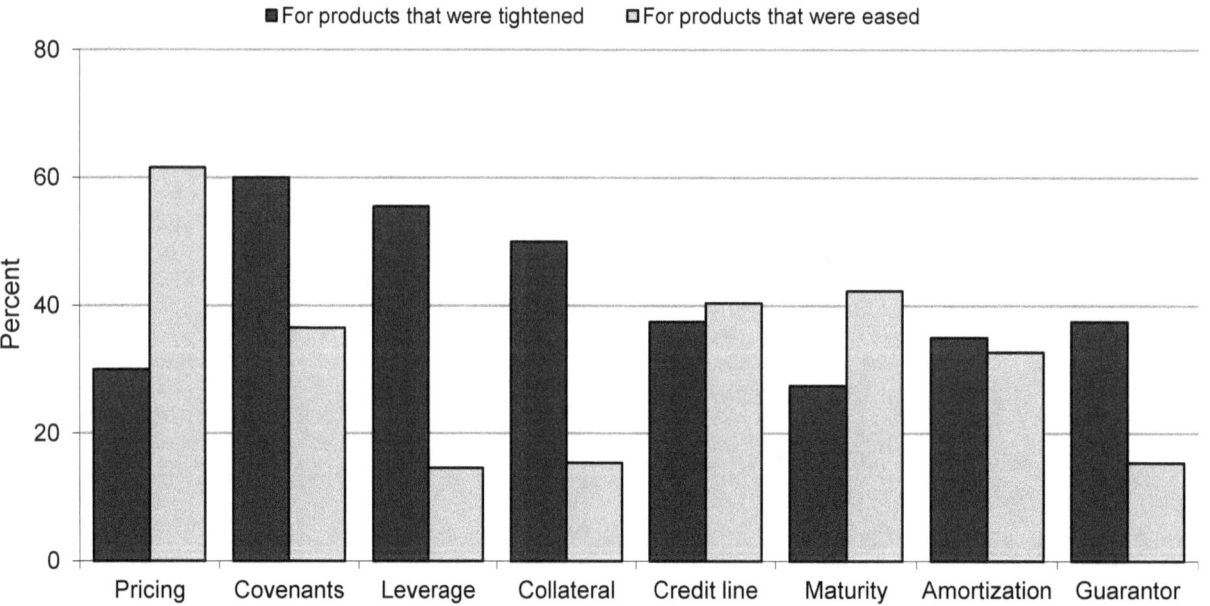

Figure 5: Commercial Credit Risk—Direction of Change and Outlook (Past 12 Months and Next 12 Months)

Past 12 months

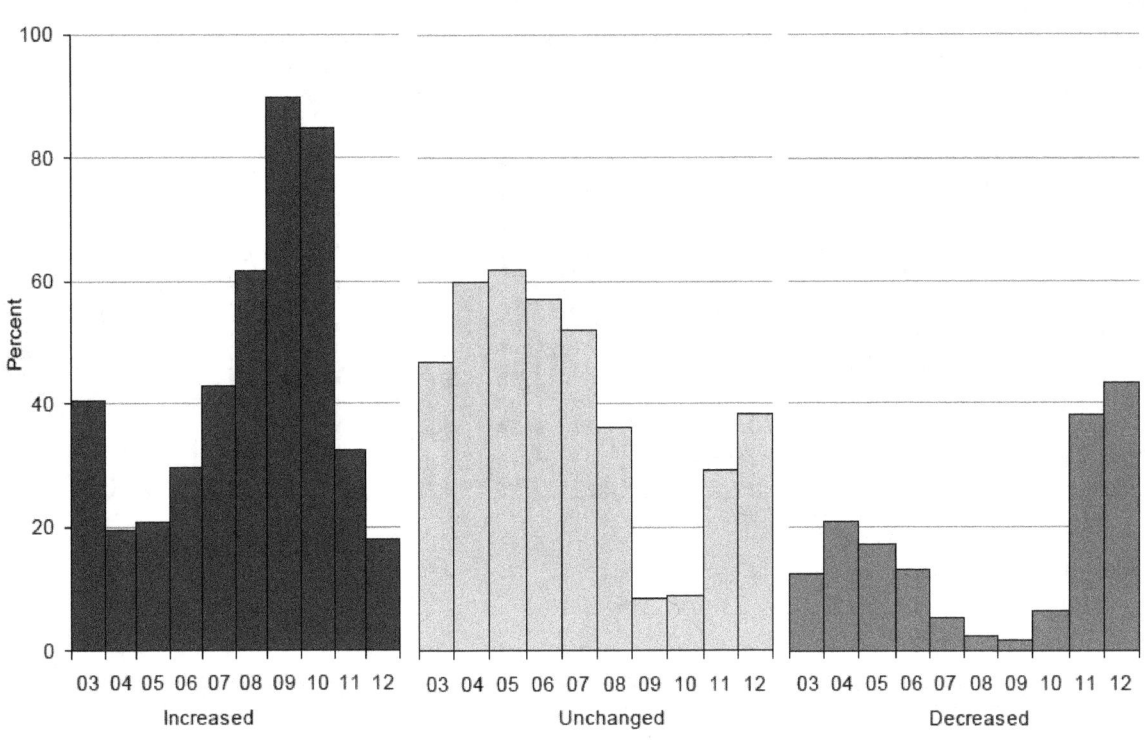

Next 12 months

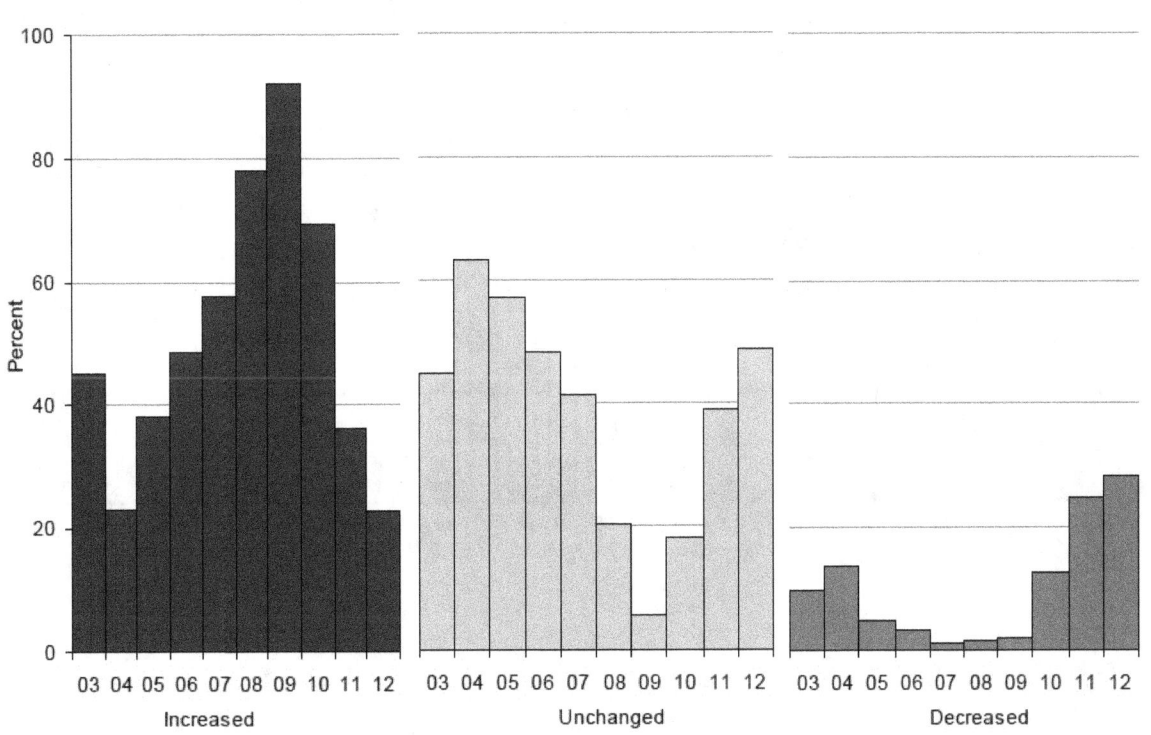

Figure 6: Commercial Credit Risk Trends—Current Credit Risk Change, by Product Type

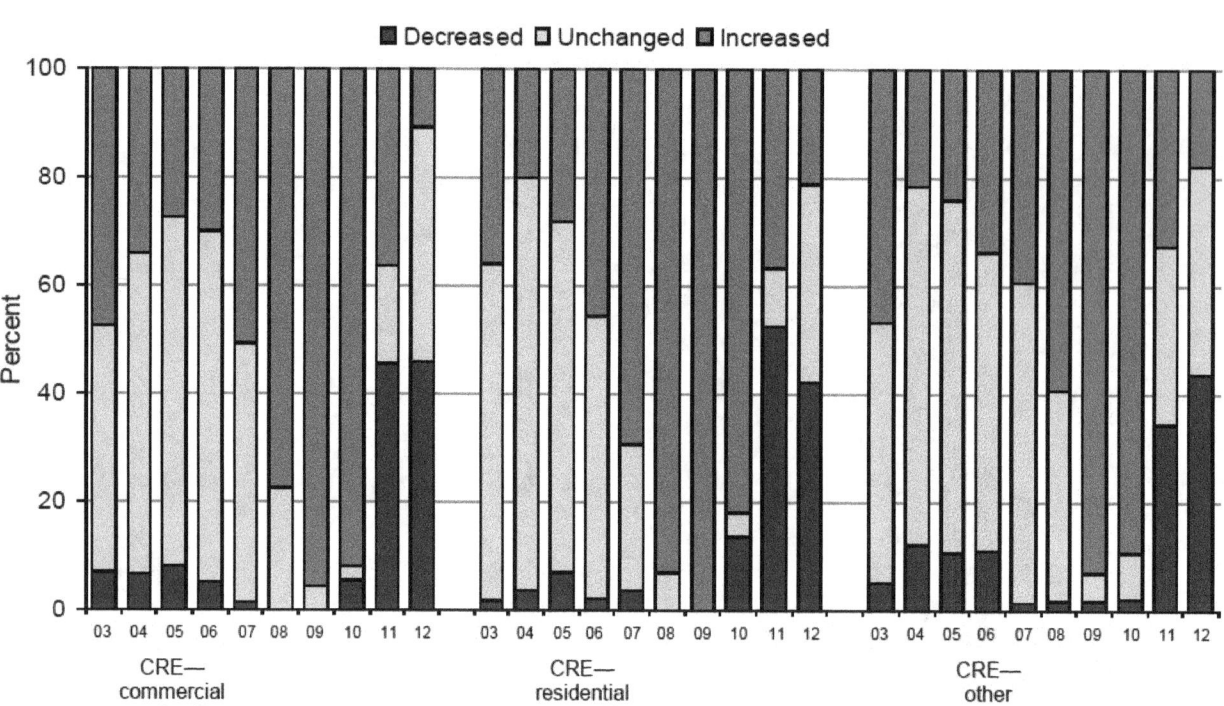

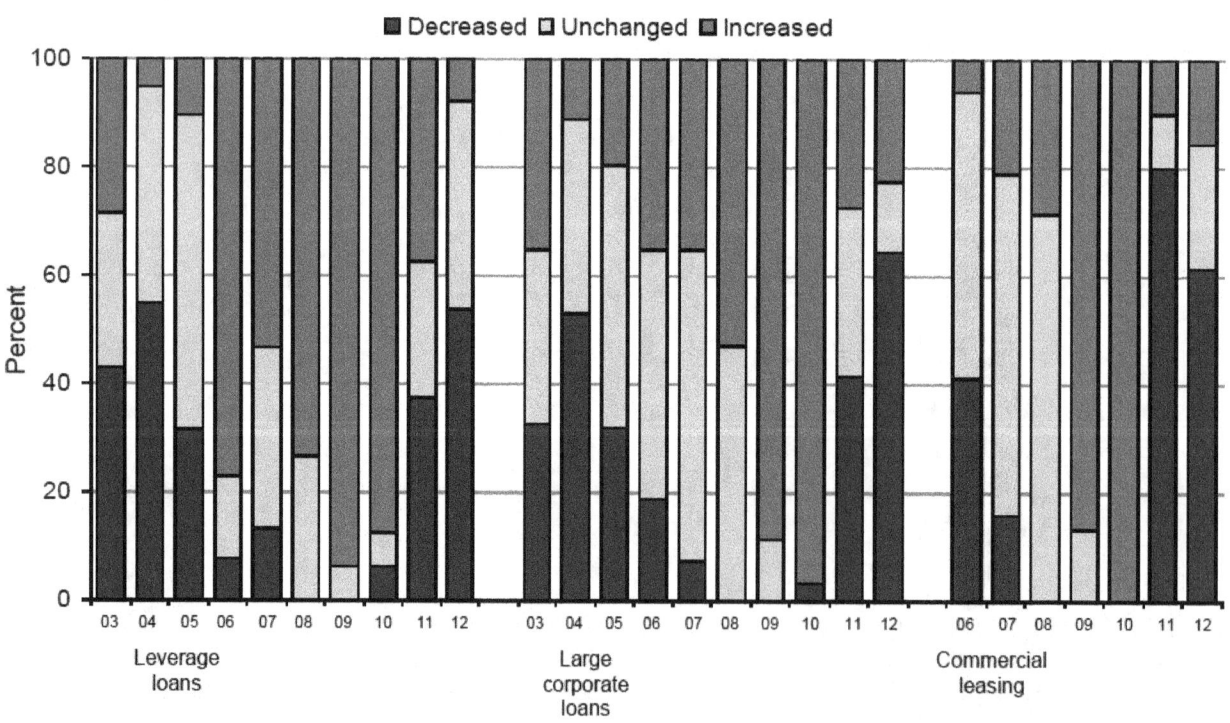

Figure 6 (cont): Commercial Credit Risk Trends—Current Credit Risk Change, by Product Type

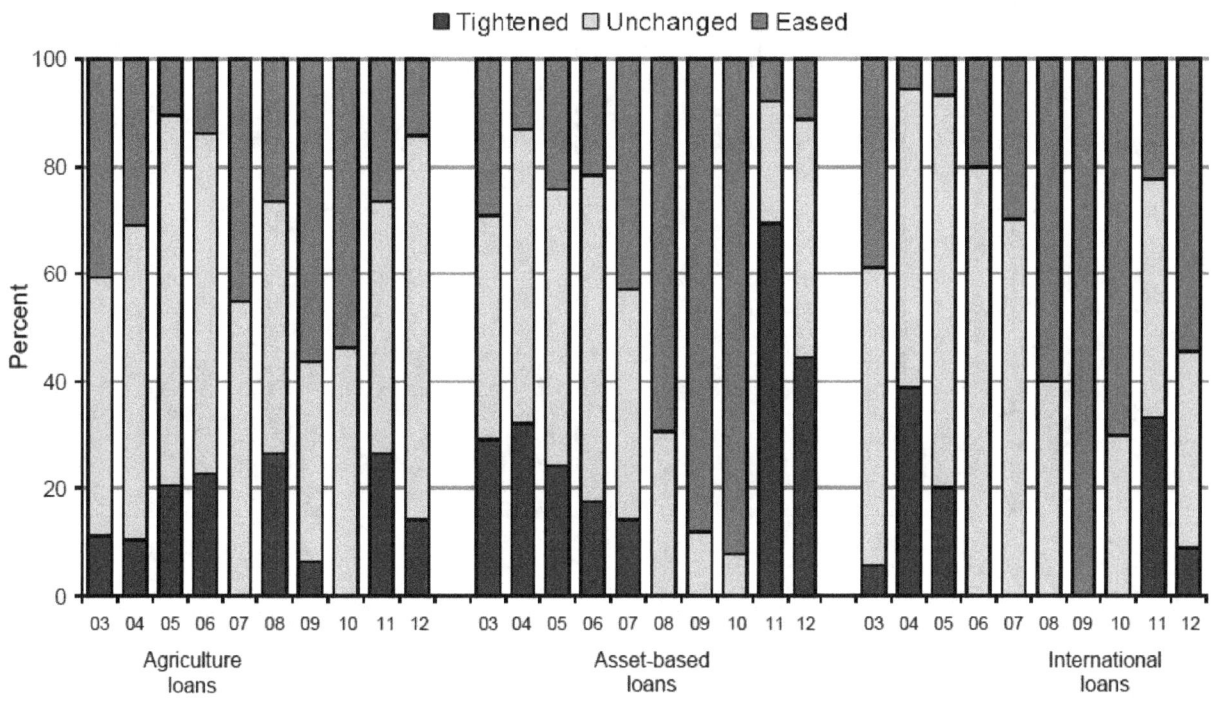

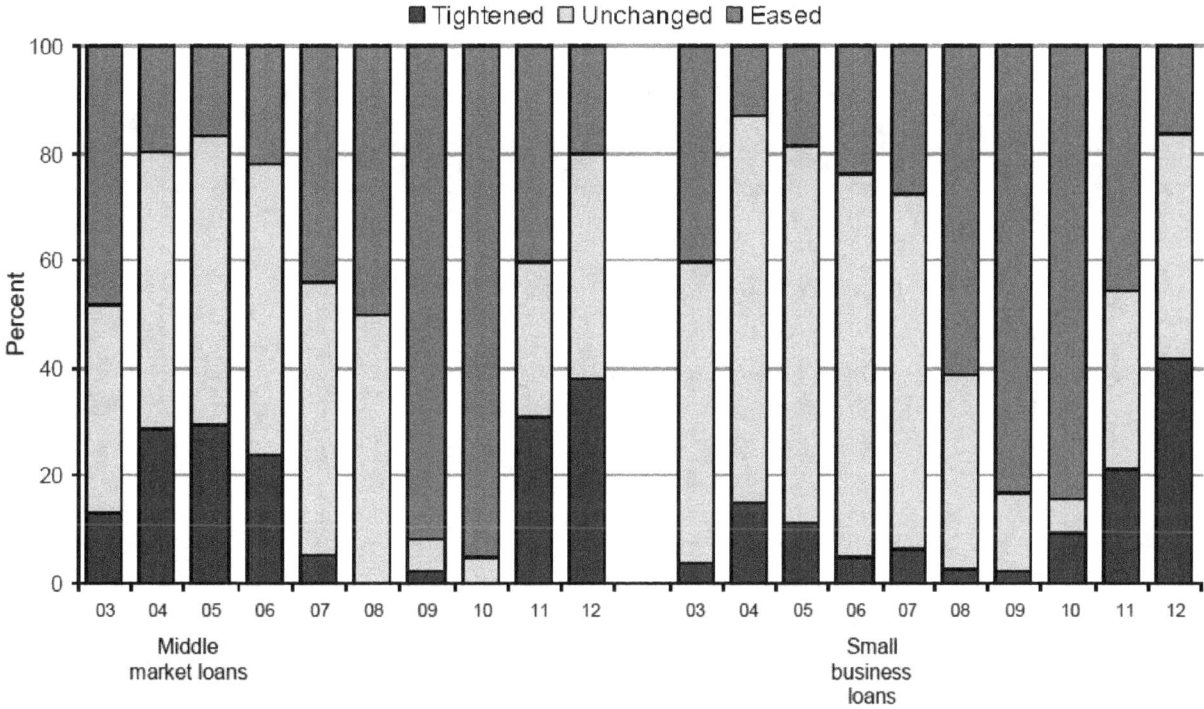

Figure 7: Credit Underwriting Trends—Retail

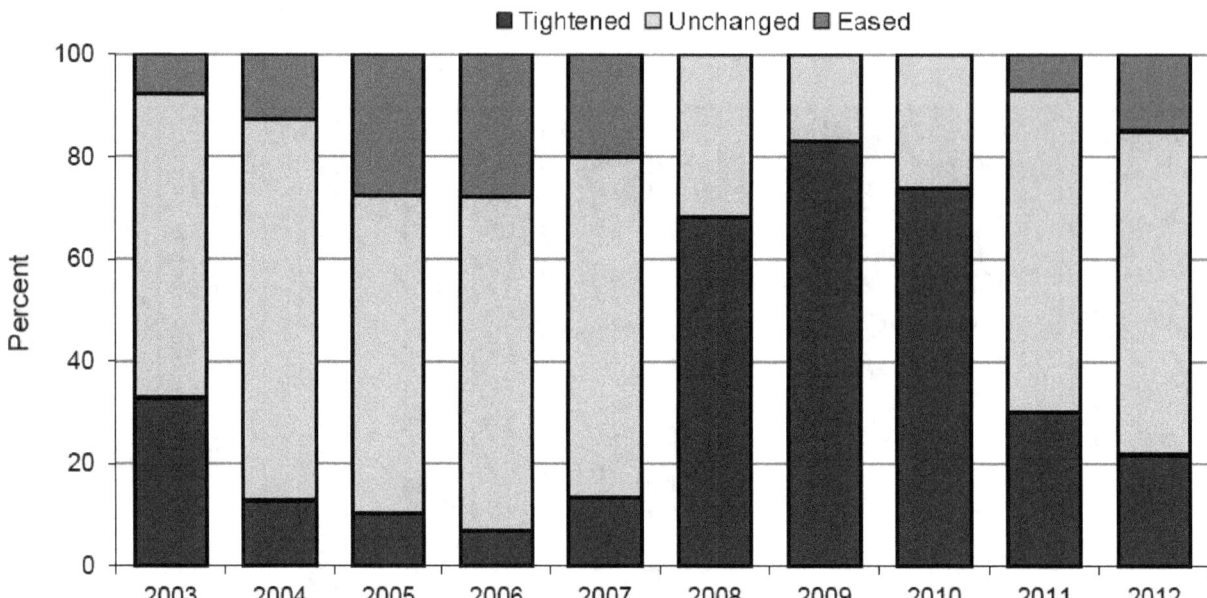

Figure 8: Retail Underwriting Trends, by Product Type

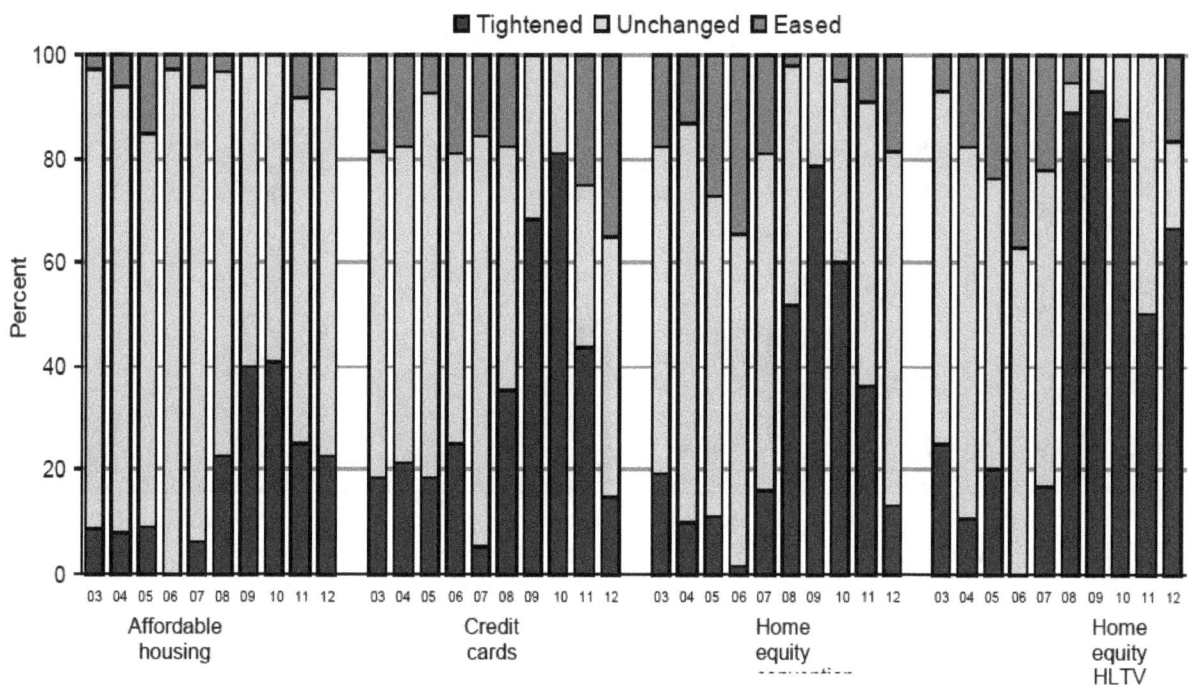

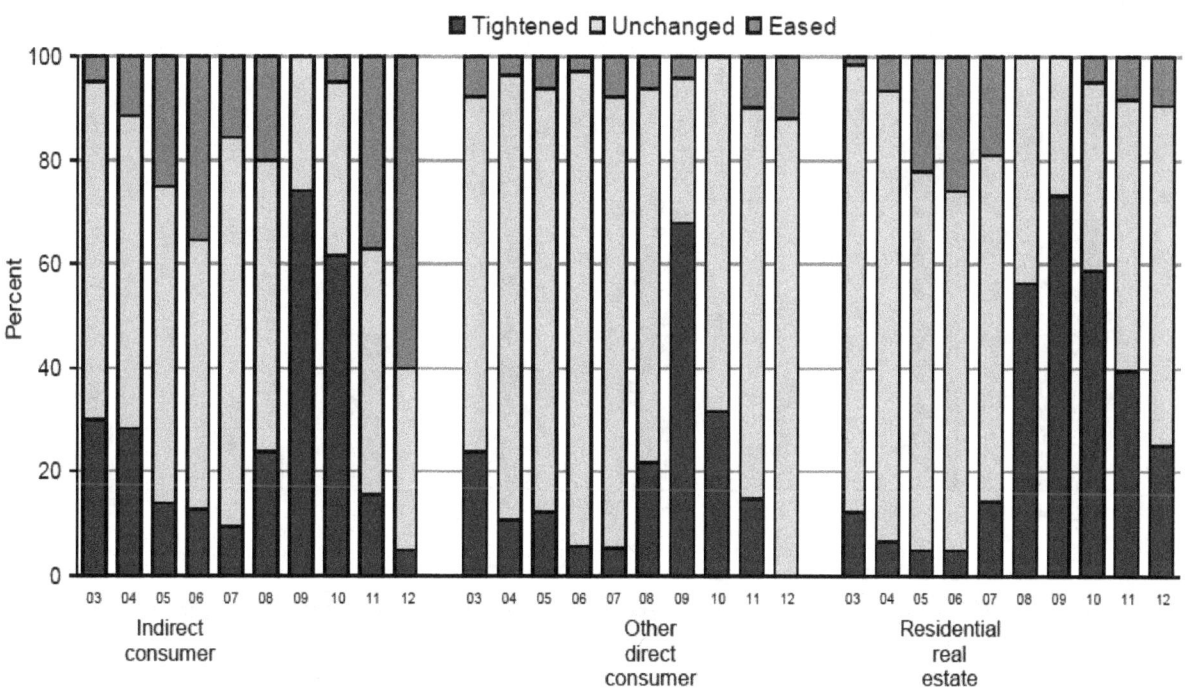

Figure 9: Reasons for Changing Retail Underwriting Standards

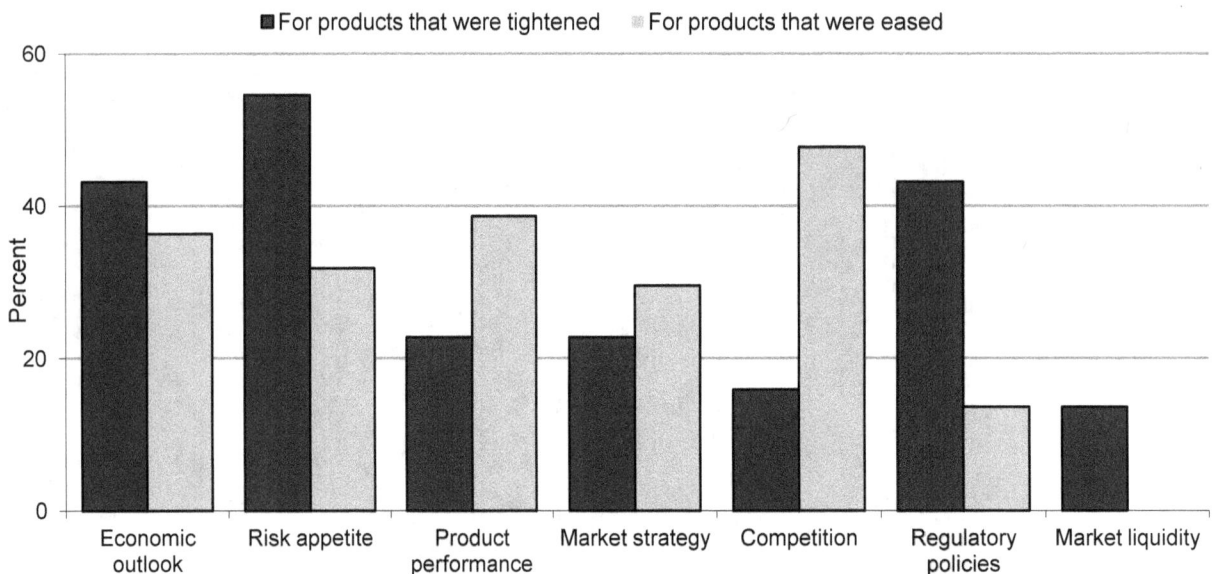

Figure 10: Overall Methods Used to Change Retail Underwriting Standards

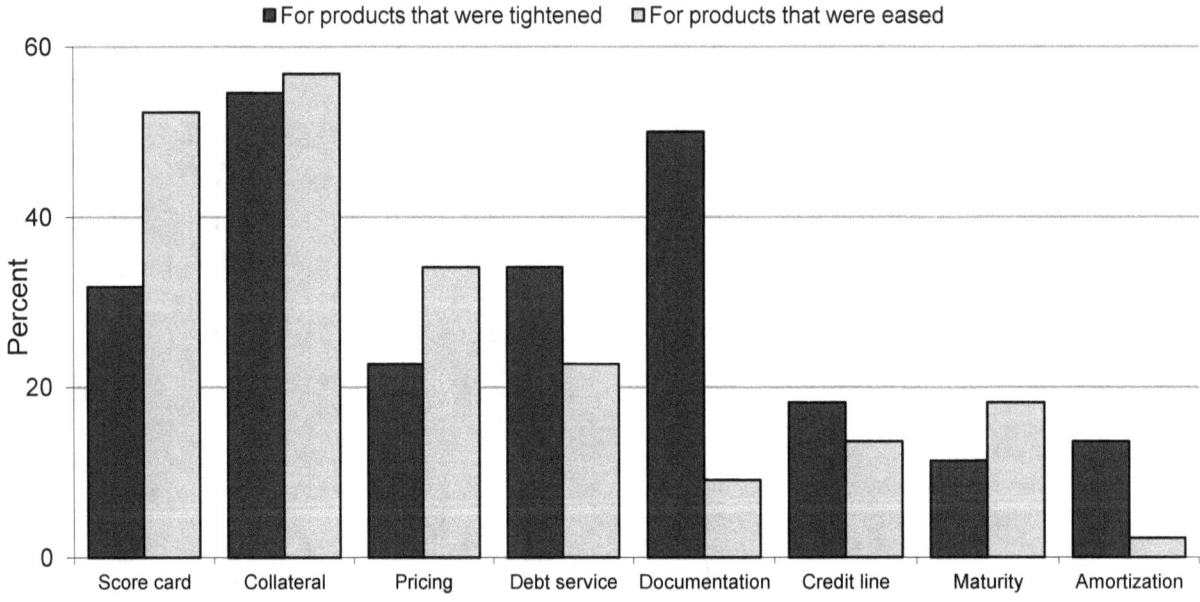

Figure 11: Retail Credit Risk Direction of Change and Outlook

Previous 12 months

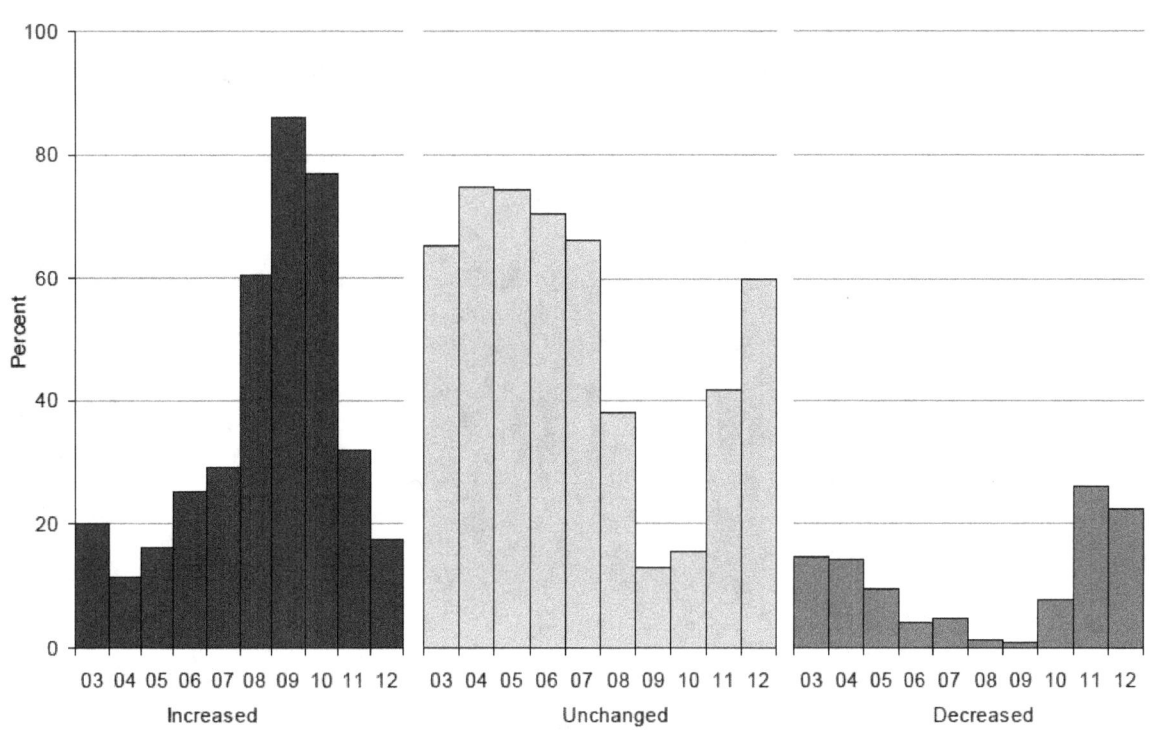

Next 12 months

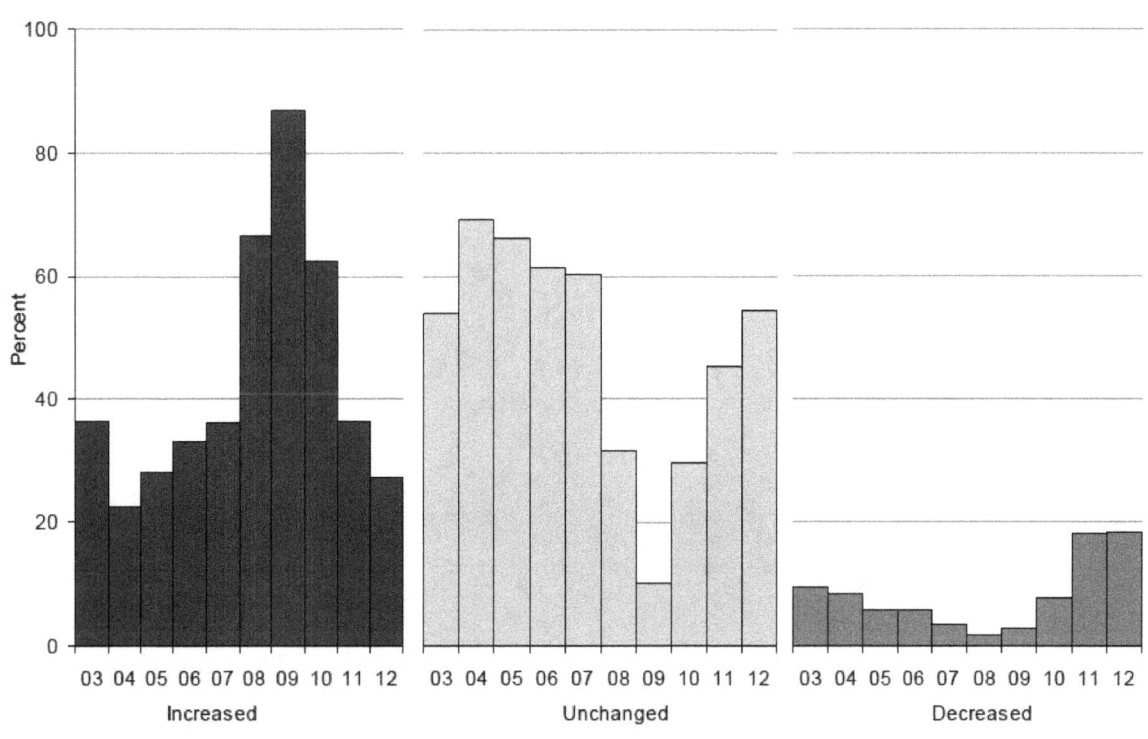

Figure 12: Retail Credit Risk Trends—Current Credit Risk Change, by Product Type

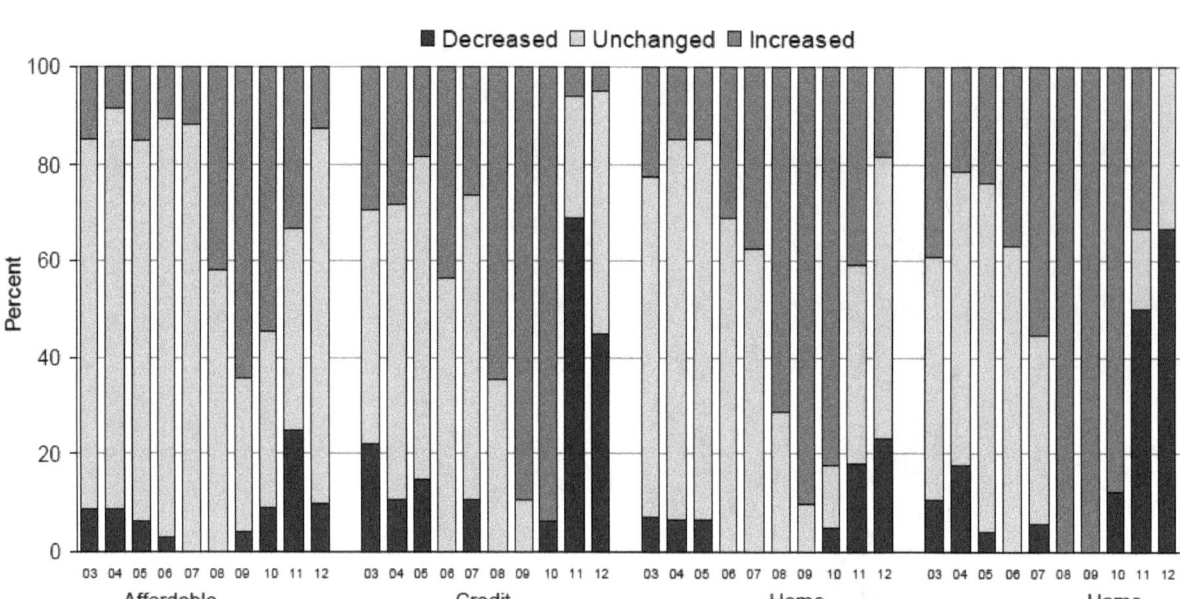

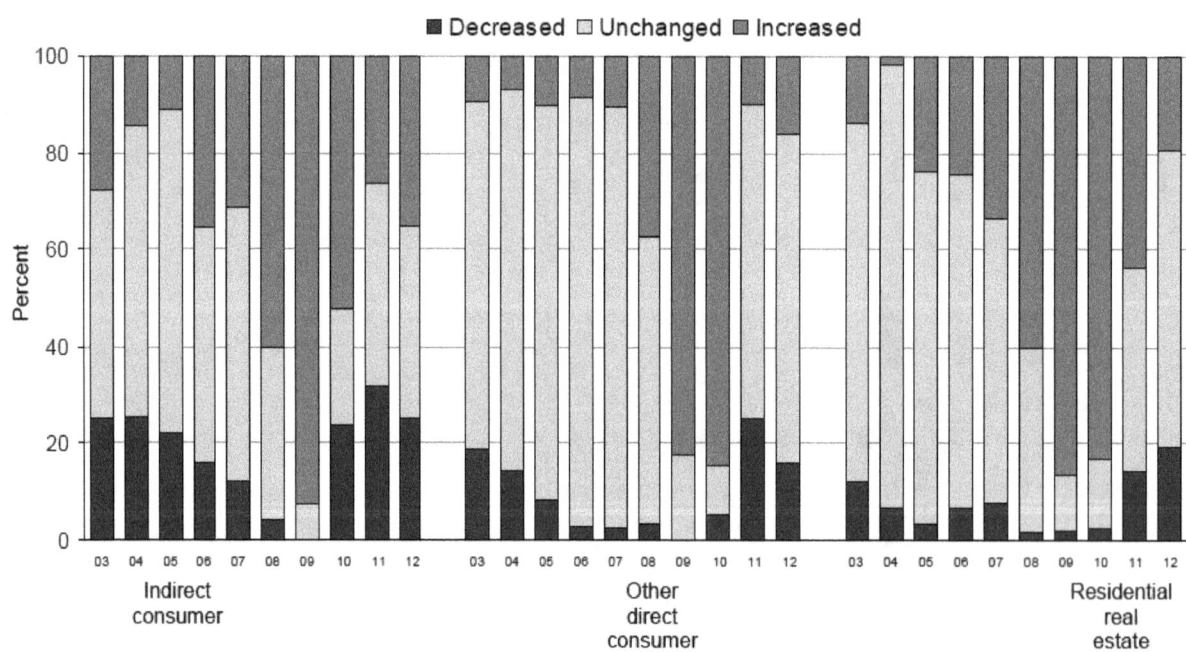

Part III: Data Tables

Some percentages in tables and figures do not add to 100 because of rounding.

A. Commercial Lending Portfolios

Agricultural Lending

Fourteen of the 87 surveyed banks met the threshold for reporting on agricultural lending.

Table 15: Changes in Underwriting Standards in Agricultural Loan Portfolios (Percentage of Responses)

Year	Eased	Unchanged	Tightened
2003	0	67	33
2004	0	93	7
2005	0	93	7
2006	5	95	0
2007	10	80	10
2008	0	95	5
2009	0	75	25
2010	0	54	46
2011	0	80	20
2012	0	79	21

Table 16: Changes in the Level of Credit Risk in Agricultural Loan Portfolios (Percentage of Responses)

Year	Declined significantly	Declined somewhat	Unchanged	Increased somewhat	Increased significantly
2003	0	11	48	41	0
2004	0	10	59	31	0
2005	4	17	69	10	0
2006	0	23	63	14	0
2007	0	0	55	45	0
2008	0	26	47	26	0
2009	0	6	38	56	0
2010	0	0	46	31	23
2011	0	27	46	27	0
2012	7	7	72	14	0
Expected risk in 12 months	0	0	57	43	0

Asset-Based Loans

Eighteen surveyed banks met the threshold for reporting on asset-based lending.

Table 17: Changes in Underwriting Standards in Asset-Based Loan Portfolios (Percentage of Responses)

Year	Eased	Unchanged	Tightened
2003	0	58	42
2004	16	71	13
2005	30	67	3
2006	30	57	13
2007	25	68	7
2008	8	70	22
2009	6	23	71
2010	8	31	61
2011	23	54	23
2012	33	61	6

Table 18: Changes in the Level of Credit Risk in Asset-Based Loan Portfolios (Percentage of Responses)

Year	Declined significantly	Declined somewhat	Unchanged	Increased somewhat	Increased significantly
2003	3	26	42	29	0
2004	3	29	55	13	0
2005	0	24	52	24	0
2006	0	17	61	22	0
2007	0	14	43	43	0
2008	0	0	30	70	0
2009	0	0	12	70	18
2010	0	0	8	77	15
2011	0	69	23	8	0
2012	11	33	45	11	0
Expected risk in 12 months	0	22	56	22	0

Commercial Leasing

Thirteen surveyed banks met the threshold for reporting on commercial leasing.

Table 19: Changes in Underwriting Standards in Commercial Leasing Loan Portfolios (Percentage of Responses)

Year	Eased	Unchanged	Tightened
2006	12	76	12
2007	26	69	5
2008	7	50	43
2009	0	40	60
2010	0	27	73
2011	10	60	30
2012	8	77	15

Table 20: Changes in the Level of Credit Risk in Commercial Leasing Loan Portfolios (Percentage of Responses)

Year	Declined significantly	Declined somewhat	Unchanged	Increased somewhat	Increased significantly
2006	6	35	53	6	0
2007	0	16	63	21	0
2008	0	0	71	29	0
2009	0	0	13	80	7
2010	0	0	0	55	45
2011	0	80	10	10	0
2012	0	62	23	15	0
Expected risk in 12 months	0	31	61	8	0

Commercial Real Estate Lending—Commercial Construction

Thirty-four surveyed banks met the threshold for reporting on commercial construction lending.

Table 21: Changes in Underwriting Standards in Commercial Construction Loan Portfolios (Percentage of Responses)

Year	Eased	Unchanged	Tightened
2003	2	61	37
2004	10	75	15
2005	29	63	8
2006	32	56	12
2007	28	59	13
2008	8	43	49
2009	0	20	80
2010	3	25	72
2011	3	61	36
2012	5	75	20

Table 22: Changes in the Level of Credit Risk in Commercial Construction Loan Portfolios (Percentage of Responses)

Year	Declined significantly	Declined somewhat	Unchanged	Increased somewhat	Increased significantly
2003	0	7	46	42	5
2004	0	7	59	34	0
2005	2	5	65	28	0
2006	0	5	65	30	0
2007	0	2	48	49	1
2008	0	0	22	69	8
2009	0	0	5	54	41
2010	0	5	3	50	42
2011	6	40	18	33	3
2012	8	38	43	8	3
Expected risk in 12 months	5	41	41	13	0

Commercial Real Estate Lending—Residential Construction

Nineteen surveyed banks met the threshold for reporting on residential construction lending.

Table 23: Changes in Underwriting Standards in Residential Construction Loan Portfolios (Percentage of Responses)

Year	Eased	Unchanged	Tightened
2003	0	76	24
2004	5	86	9
2005	21	72	7
2006	25	64	11
2007	17	50	33
2008	2	36	62
2009	0	8	92
2010	0	36	64
2011	0	63	37
2012	0	79	21

Table 24: Changes in the Level of Credit Risk in Residential Construction Loan Portfolios (Percentage of Responses)

Year	Declined significantly	Declined somewhat	Unchanged	Increased somewhat	Increased significantly
2003	0	2	62	34	2
2004	0	4	76	18	2
2005	2	6	65	27	0
2006	0	2	52	46	0
2007	0	4	27	63	6
2008	0	0	7	48	45
2009	0	0	0	34	66
2010	5	9	4	41	41
2011	5	47	11	32	5
2012	10	32	37	21	0
Expected risk in 12 months	5	26	53	16	0

Commercial Real Estate Lending—Other

Seventy-three surveyed banks met the threshold for reporting on other commercial real estate lending.

Table 25: Changes in Underwriting Standards in Other Commercial Real Estate Loan Portfolios (Percentage of Responses)

Year	Eased	Unchanged	Tightened
2003	5	71	24
2004	8	83	9
2005	24	65	11
2006	32	60	8
2007	20	73	7
2008	2	73	25
2009	2	22	76
2010	2	38	60
2011	9	58	33
2012	12	76	12

Table 26: Changes in the Level of Credit Risk in Other Commercial Real Estate Loan Portfolios (Percentage of Responses)

Year	Declined significantly	Declined somewhat	Unchanged	Increased somewhat	Increased significantly
2003	0	5	48	43	4
2004	0	12	66	20	2
2005	2	9	65	24	0
2006	1	10	55	34	0
2007	0	2	59	38	1
2008	0	2	38	58	2
2009	0	2	5	67	26
2010	0	2	9	55	34
2011	2	33	33	23	9
2012	8	36	38	15	3
Expected risk in 12 months	0	43	41	16	0

International Lending

Eleven surveyed banks met the threshold for reporting on international lending.

Table 27: Changes in Underwriting Standards in International Loan Portfolios (Percentage of Responses)

Year	Eased	Unchanged	Tightened
2003	6	55	39
2004	11	61	28
2005	27	73	0
2006	30	70	0
2007	30	70	0
2008	10	60	30
2009	0	13	87
2010	30	40	30
2011	56	33	11
2012	36	36	27

Table 28: Changes in the Level of Credit Risk in International Loan Portfolios (Percentage of Responses)

Year	Declined significantly	Declined somewhat	Unchanged	Increased somewhat	Increased significantly
2003	0	6	55	33	6
2004	6	33	55	6	0
2005	0	20	73	7	0
2006	0	0	80	20	0
2007	0	0	70	30	0
2008	0	0	40	40	20
2009	0	0	0	63	37
2010	0	0	30	50	20
2011	0	33	45	22	0
2012	0	9	36	55	0
Expected risk in 12 months	0	0	55	45	0

Large Corporate Loans

Thirty-one surveyed banks met the threshold for reporting on large corporate loans.

Table 29: Changes in Underwriting Standards in Large Corporate Loan Portfolios (Percentage of Responses)

Year	Eased	Unchanged	Tightened
2003	3	49	48
2004	17	66	17
2005	32	68	0
2006	49	51	0
2007	40	60	0
2008	6	62	32
2009	0	40	60
2010	3	38	59
2011	38	55	7
2012	32	58	10

Table 30: Changes in the Level of Credit Risk in Large Corporate Loan Portfolios (Percentage of Responses)

Year	Declined significantly	Declined somewhat	Unchanged	Increased somewhat	Increased significantly
2003	5	27	33	30	5
2004	17	36	36	11	0
2005	5	27	49	19	0
2006	0	19	46	32	3
2007	0	8	57	35	0
2008	0	0	47	47	6
2009	0	0	12	77	11
2010	0	3	0	76	21
2011	0	41	31	28	0
2012	10	55	13	19	3
Expected risk in 12 months	0	23	42	35	0

Leveraged Loans

Thirteen surveyed banks met the threshold for reporting on leveraged loans.

Table 31: Changes in Underwriting Standards in Leveraged Loan Portfolios (Percentage of Responses)

Year	Eased	Unchanged	Tightened
2003	0	48	52
2004	15	85	0
2005	32	68	0
2006	61	31	8
2007	67	33	0
2008	20	20	60
2009	0	31	69
2010	0	25	75
2011	37	44	19
2012	38	62	0

Table 32: Changes in the Level of Credit Risk in Leveraged Loan Portfolios (Percentage of Responses)

Year	Declined significantly	Declined somewhat	Unchanged	Increased somewhat	Increased significantly
2003	10	33	28	29	0
2004	15	40	40	5	0
2005	5	27	58	5	5
2006	0	8	15	69	8
2007	0	13	34	53	0
2008	0	0	27	53	20
2009	0	0	6	63	31
2010	0	6	6	63	25
2011	0	38	25	31	6
2012	8	46	38	8	0
Expected risk in 12 months	0	23	39	38	0

Middle Market Lending

Forty-nine surveyed banks met the threshold for reporting on middle market lending.

**Table 33: Changes in Underwriting Standards in Middle Market Loan Portfolios
(Percentage of Responses)**

Year	Eased	Unchanged	Tightened
2003	6	63	31
2004	14	81	5
2005	28	67	5
2006	31	66	3
2007	33	60	7
2008	6	69	25
2009	0	33	67
2010	0	50	50
2011	19	64	17
2012	22	70	8

**Table 34: Changes in the Level of Credit Risk in Middle Market Loan Portfolios
(Percentage of Responses)**

Year	Declined significantly	Declined somewhat	Unchanged	Increased somewhat	Increased significantly
2003	0	13	39	44	4
2004	0	28	52	18	2
2005	4	26	54	16	0
2006	0	24	54	20	2
2007	0	5	51	44	0
2008	0	0	50	48	2
2009	0	2	6	88	4
2010	0	0	5	73	22
2011	0	31	29	38	2
2012	4	34	42	16	4
Expected risk in 12 months	0	20	50	28	2

Small Business Lending

Forty-four surveyed banks met the threshold for reporting on small business lending.

Table 35: Changes in Underwriting Standards in Small Business Loan Portfolios (Percentage of Responses)

Year	Eased	Unchanged	Tightened
2003	4	65	31
2004	11	74	15
2005	13	81	6
2006	19	76	5
2007	11	76	13
2008	11	72	17
2009	0	36	64
2010	0	34	66
2011	12	55	33
2012	9	82	9

Table 36: Changes in the Level of Credit Risk in Small Business Loan Portfolios (Percentage of Responses)

Year	Declined significantly	Declined somewhat	Unchanged	Increased somewhat	Increased significantly
2003	0	4	56	38	2
2004	0	15	72	13	0
2005	0	11	70	19	0
2006	0	5	71	22	2
2007	2	4	66	26	2
2008	0	3	36	58	3
2009	0	2	14	72	12
2010	0	9	6	66	19
2011	0	21	33	46	0
2012	2	40	42	16	0
Expected risk in 12 months	0	21	63	16	0

B. Retail Lending Portfolios

Affordable Housing Lending

Thirty surveyed banks met the threshold for reporting on affordable housing lending.

Table 37: Changes in Underwriting Standards in Affordable Housing Loan Portfolios (Percentage of Responses)

Year	Eased	Unchanged	Tightened
2003	3	88	9
2004	6	86	8
2005	15	76	9
2006	3	97	0
2007	6	88	6
2008	3	74	23
2009	0	60	40
2010	0	59	41
2011	8	67	25
2012	6	71	23

Table 38: Changes in the Level of Credit Risk in Affordable Housing Loan Portfolios (Percentage of Responses)

Year	Declined significantly	Declined somewhat	Unchanged	Increased somewhat	Increased significantly
2003	0	9	76	15	0
2004	0	9	82	9	0
2005	0	6	79	15	0
2006	0	3	86	11	0
2007	0	0	88	12	0
2008	0	0	58	35	6
2009	0	4	32	52	12
2010	0	9	36	46	9
2011	0	25	42	33	0
2012	0	10	77	13	0
Expected risk in 12 months	0	13	64	23	0

Conventional Home Equity Lending

Sixty surveyed banks met the threshold for reporting on conventional home equity lending.

Table 39: Changes in Underwriting Standards in Conventional Home Equity Loan Portfolios (Percentage of Responses)

Year	Eased	Unchanged	Tightened
2003	18	63	19
2004	13	77	10
2005	27	62	11
2006	34	64	2
2007	19	65	16
2008	2	46	52
2009	0	22	78
2010	5	35	60
2011	9	55	36
2012	18	68	14

Table 40: Changes in the Level of Credit Risk in Conventional Home Equity Loan Portfolios (Percentage of Responses)

Year	Declined significantly	Declined somewhat	Unchanged	Increased somewhat	Increased significantly
2003	4	4	69	23	0
2004	0	6	79	13	2
2005	0	7	78	15	0
2006	0	0	69	29	2
2007	0	0	63	34	3
2008	0	0	29	52	19
2009	0	0	10	63	27
2010	0	5	12	73	10
2011	0	18	41	41	0
2012	0	23	58	18	0
Expected risk in 12 months	0	28	50	22	0

Credit Card Lending

Twenty surveyed banks met the threshold for reporting on credit card lending.

Table 41: Changes in Underwriting Standards in Credit Card Loan Portfolios (Percentage of Responses)

Year	Eased	Unchanged	Tightened
2003	19	62	19
2004	18	61	21
2005	7	74	19
2006	19	56	25
2007	16	79	5
2008	18	47	35
2009	0	32	68
2010	0	19	81
2011	25	31	44
2012	35	50	15

Table 42: Changes in the Level of Credit Risk in Credit Card Loan Portfolios (Percentage of Responses)

Year	Declined significantly	Declined somewhat	Unchanged	Increased somewhat	Increased significantly
2003	0	22	48	30	0
2004	0	11	61	25	3
2005	0	15	67	18	0
2006	0	0	56	44	0
2007	0	11	63	26	0
2008	0	0	35	65	0
2009	0	0	10	53	37
2010	0	6	0	63	31
2011	0	69	25	0	6
2012	15	30	50	5	0
Expected risk in 12 months	0	5	60	35	0

Direct Consumer Lending

Twenty-five surveyed banks met the threshold for reporting on other direct consumer lending.

Table 43: Changes in Underwriting Standards in Other Direct Consumer Loan Portfolios (Percentage of Responses)

Year	Eased	Unchanged	Tightened
2003	8	68	24
2004	3	86	11
2005	6	82	12
2006	3	91	6
2007	8	87	5
2008	6	72	22
2009	4	28	68
2010	0	68	32
2011	10	75	15
2012	12	88	0

Table 44: Changes in the Level of Credit Risk in Other Direct Consumer Loan Portfolios (Percentage of Responses)

Year	Declined significantly	Declined somewhat	Unchanged	Increased somewhat	Increased significantly
2003	2	17	72	7	2
2004	2	13	78	7	0
2005	0	8	82	10	0
2006	0	3	88	9	0
2007	0	3	87	10	0
2008	0	3	59	38	0
2009	0	0	18	68	14
2010	0	5	11	74	10
2011	0	25	65	10	0
2012	4	12	68	16	0
Expected risk in 12 months	0	0	88	12	0

High Loan-to-Value Home Equity Lending

Six surveyed banks met the threshold for reporting on HLTV home equity lending.

Table 45: Changes in Underwriting Standards in HLTV Home Equity Loan Portfolios (Percentage of Responses)

Year	Eased	Unchanged	Tightened
2003	7	68	25
2004	18	71	11
2005	24	56	20
2006	37	63	0
2007	22	61	17
2008	6	6	89
2009	0	7	93
2010	0	13	87
2011	0	50	50
2012	17	17	66

Table 46: Changes in the Level of Credit Risk in HLTV Home Equity Loan Portfolios (Percentage of Responses)

Year	Declined significantly	Declined somewhat	Unchanged	Increased somewhat	Increased significantly
2003	0	11	50	36	3
2004	0	18	61	18	3
2005	0	4	72	24	0
2006	0	0	63	37	0
2007	0	6	39	55	0
2008	0	0	0	56	44
2009	0	0	0	36	64
2010	0	13	0	50	37
2011	17	33	17	33	0
2012	0	67	33	0	0
Expected risk in 12 months	0	50	33	17	0

Indirect Consumer Lending

Twenty surveyed banks met the threshold for reporting on indirect consumer lending.

Table 47: Changes in Underwriting Standards in Indirect Consumer Loan Portfolios (Percentage of Responses)

Year	Eased	Unchanged	Tightened
2003	5	65	30
2004	11	60	29
2005	25	61	14
2006	35	52	13
2007	16	75	9
2008	20	56	24
2009	0	26	74
2010	5	33	62
2011	37	47	16
2012	60	35	5

Table 48: Changes in the Level of Credit Risk in Indirect Consumer Loan Portfolios (Percentage of Responses)

Year	Declined significantly	Declined somewhat	Unchanged	Increased somewhat	Increased significantly
2003	5	20	47	28	0
2004	0	26	60	14	0
2005	3	19	67	8	3
2006	6	10	48	36	0
2007	0	3	87	10	0
2008	0	4	36	60	0
2009	0	0	7	74	19
2010	0	24	24	47	5
2011	0	32	42	26	0
2012	0	25	40	35	0
Expected risk in 12 months	0	10	45	45	0

Residential Real Estate Lending

Eighty-four surveyed banks met the threshold for reporting on residential real estate lending.

Table 49: Changes in Underwriting Standards in Residential Real Estate Loan Portfolios (Percentage of Responses)

Year	Eased	Unchanged	Tightened
2003	2	86	12
2004	7	86	7
2005	22	73	5
2006	26	69	5
2007	19	67	14
2008	0	44	56
2009	0	27	73
2010	5	36	59
2011	8	52	40
2012	10	65	25

Table 50: Changes in the Level of Credit Risk in Residential Real Estate Loan Portfolios (Percentage of Responses)

Year	Declined significantly	Declined somewhat	Unchanged	Increased somewhat	Increased significantly
2003	0	12	74	12	2
2004	0	6	92	2	0
2005	0	3	73	24	0
2006	0	7	69	24	0
2007	2	6	59	33	0
2008	2	0	38	55	5
2009	0	2	12	69	17
2010	0	3	14	57	26
2011	0	15	42	39	4
2012	1	18	62	19	0
Expected risk in 12 months	0	22	46	32	0